MEETING THE OCCULT

MEETING THE OTHERS

MEETING
THE OCCULT

by

BASIL WILBY

LUTTERWORTH EDUCATIONAL

GUILDFORD AND LONDON

First published 1974

LUTTERWORTH EDUCATIONAL · GUILDFORD & LONDON

ISBN 0 7188 2045 2

Printed in Great Britain by The Bowering Press, Plymouth

CONTENTS

1

WHAT SPIRITUALISTS
AND OCCULTISTS BELIEVE

The Heaven Worlds

'WHERE do we go when we die?' This question is asked sooner or later by every thinking person. And it is this question that the Spiritualists claim to answer, and in the most direct way possible—by personal experience!

They believe it is possible to communicate with the dead. In fact, they prefer not to refer to people as being 'dead'. They say that they have 'passed over' or are 'in spirit'. Passed over, that is, to another form of existence, as spirits.

This other form of existence is, in most cases, very much like our own. People the other side of death seem to live in houses, to have towns and countryside, friends and relations, although generally in much more pleasant conditions than are known to us in the physical world. Therefore these realms are often called 'heaven worlds', or are referred to as the 'astral plane', as opposed to the physical plane upon which we live.

So similar, in fact, are many of the descriptions of life after death to the life we know on the physical plane that some critics have accused the spiritualists of 'suburbanising' the astral plane.

To this, spiritualists reply that it is only natural to expect this similarity. When people 'pass over' they become free of the physical body and live entirely on levels of mind. This allows them to have what they choose in their surroundings.

Just as we on the physical plane are free to make fantasies within our own minds, so are they on the astral plane, but with them the fantasy is real. If they desire plum pudding, lo, a plum pudding appears! If they wish to dwell in a pleasant detached house in a nice neighbourhood, then house and neighbourhood duly appear.

Whilst some would choose to live in somewhat out of the way conditions, in summery woods, or in a kind of science fiction city full of futuristic devices, the great majority will prefer to live lives much as they have been used to, though with the pains and frustrations removed.

There is certainly a great superficial attraction about such a picture of life after death. It seems almost too good to be true. Perhaps it is. For there crops up an obvious snag. Suppose Aunt Edna delights in coming to see you but you don't much relish the sight of her? To be summoned up to appear in Aunt Edna's heaven world any time she wanted to see you, or to have her suddenly appearing without warning in yours, could be disconcerting, not to say embarrassing.

The difficulty is explained, however, by the theory that you do not in fact see her unless you want to. Should you not want to, then what she in fact converses with is but an animated picture of you. She is quite satisfied and you are not bothered.

On reflection, however, there seems to be something not quite right here. For this to happen, everyone must be living in his own dream world, more or less in solitary confinement. Real communication, though not impossible, would be an uncertain business, for you would never really know if you were in touch with another person or with an image of your own making. This problem, in fact, runs right through all matters of spiritualist communications, including those between this world and the next.

Most spiritualists would hasten to add that there are many levels of existence on 'the other side', and that, whilst most souls live in this condition of having all they desire for a certain time, this eventually begins to pall. The soul begins to realize that this is not really the means to a deeply satisfying happiness.

Following upon this realization, the soul begins to change its conditions of existence and moves on to higher heaven worlds. There are not many descriptions of these higher states, partly because they are apparently too abstract to be described in earthly terms, and partly because souls in these higher conditions find communication with those on earth more difficult, or even impossible.

Some souls, it is said, have a certain senior status, or sense of mission, to help others to make this transition to higher worlds. These are generally called 'guides' and perform a similar function to the traditional 'guardian angel'. The 'guides' are particularly helpful to those who have newly 'passed over', especially if this was very sudden. With sudden or violent death it can apparently happen that the person does not realize that he or she is 'dead'. Similarly, to pass over under drugs, under hospital anaesthetic for instance, means that people may be in some state of confusion on finding themselves in a world so similar to and yet so different from the one they have known.

Some spiritualists make a practice of trying to help such souls, in conjunction with some of the astral 'guides'. This is particularly so in times of war.

Such rescue operations may also be attempted to release souls from the 'lower hells'. In these are the obsessively wicked and the unfortunates who have found life too much for them and committed suicide. The hell they are in is not a place of fire and brimstone and deliberate punishment, as medieval Christians believed, but a hell of their own making. So obsessed are they with their own perverted desires or paralysing grief that they are confined in a perpetual nightmare. The task in each case is to try to break in to the vortex of self-inflicted obsession by means of love and companionship. It is rather akin to the work of the Samaritans on the physical plane. It is a specialized task, and only spiritualists of some experience and emotional balance are encouraged to take part in it.

Mediumship and Clairvoyance

The means of contact with the 'spirit worlds' is through the mind, and some are better at making this contact than others. Those that are particularly good at it are called clairvoyants, or mediums.

A clairvoyant is one who is able, by natural ability and training, to 'see' spirits with the inner eye. A clairaudient, on the other hand, 'hears' them with the inner ear. There are some, of course, who combine both functions. The term 'medium' is sometimes used to describe a clairvoyant or clairaudient, but strictly speaking a medium is one who allows his or her body to be used by a spirit, either in or out of trance.

Trance is a condition where consciousness is temporarily disconnected from the body. Under certain conditions, another being can take over and talk through the medium's vocal chords. A specialized extension of this is the type of medium who has a particular kind of nervous constitution that allows the giving off of a strange force or substance called 'ectoplasm'. This is rather like a white mist, and it can be formed into shapes by the power of thought. It can thus be used, either to build up a whole ghost figure, or to form spirit hands or rods that are able to move light objects such as tambourines, bells, paper trumpets and the like. The cabinet that is sometimes used in this type of spiritualist meeting (or 'séance'), and in which the medium may sit, is for the purpose of concentrating this ectoplasm.

There have been some very remarkable mediums capable of producing astounding phenomena, but the condition is rare. There have also been many recorded instances of such phenomena being faked, but this does not disprove genuine instances. Most mediums, however, to use the term in its widest sense, simply try nowadays to develop their telepathic powers of inner sight, sound and sense. That is, to have an impressionable imagination.

A typical spiritualist church service consists of a number of hymns, readings and prayers, such as might take place in any church or chapel. But there are two main differences. Instead of a sermon there will be an address by the medium, which may be given in a state of light trance, but this is hardly ever noticeable. Then, at the end, there is a 'clairvoyant demonstration' where the clairvoyant talks to members of the congregation and gives messages to them from various spirits.

The main object of this procedure is to give personal proof of the survival of personality after death. Mediums usually work on a circuit basis; that is, they go to a different spiritualist church each week, so each church has a different clairvoyant each week. Most give impressive performances in their fluency, speed and matter-of-fact delivery.

These public meetings are not 'spooky' in any way. They are held in bright light and in the company of a large number of people. Such conditions are not the best, however, for more personal communication, and those who wish to make closer, less public, contact with particular friends or relatives who have 'passed over', can arrange to meet in private or semi-public circles. These consist of just a few people in conditions of seclusion, quietness and semi-darkness.

In these, the medium may go into full trance, and there may be physical manifestations of a minor kind, such as raps or bells. The emphasis, however, is on communication rather than on the production of ectoplasmic parlour tricks.

Spiritualist churches also often run 'development circles'. Here you may go to see if you can develop any clairvoyant or mediumistic powers yourself. This consists largely of sitting in a condition of physical and mental passivity seeing what impressions come to you and if they are likely to be spirit communications.

Another activity is 'absent healing', whereby healing thoughts or prayers are directed upon the sick, aided, it is believed, by helpers on the astral plane. The healing does not have to be absent of course, and some practitioners find they have a gift for it and may establish spiritualist 'clinics'. Here we are getting very close to faith healing, which may take place within or outside the jurisdiction of the orthodox churches. The spiritualist healers tend to think that they are helped by deceased doctors and surgeons on 'the other side'.

Home Circles

A number of people, whether confirmed spiritualists or those on the fringes, go in for 'home circles'. These usually consist of table tapping or the use of the planchette or the ouija board.

With table tapping or table turning, those present sit in a circle, their hands spread out and touching on a light table. The table may then begin to rock, or tap, and messages may be rapped out laboriously by means of a simple agreed code, such as one rap for Yes, two raps for No, or counting raps through the alphabet.

Less laborious is the ouija board, which is perhaps better known in its more improvised form of an upturned glass on a polished table with letters of the alphabet written on pieces of paper distributed around the edge. Those present place one finger on the glass which usually begins to move and, hopefully, to spell out messages by moving from one letter to another.

Even this is a lengthy means of sending or receiving messages, and the planchette may be used. This is a small heart-shaped device supported on two wheels and a pencil point which will move around easily, making marks, on a large sheet of paper, Those present put their fingers on it and it may then begin to scribble, draw or write.

In all these methods the motive power comes, of course, from the sitters physically present. Spirits wishing to communicate do so, if they can, by manipulating the direction of force applied via the fingers through action upon the subconscious minds and automatic nervous systems of the sitters. This cannot be very easy, and frequently only rubbish is achieved by these methods unless the sitters are experienced or have a medium amongst them. Most spiritualists of any responsibility would abhor the casual use of such devices, particularly in the giggling party spirit in which they are often indulged.

Whilst the whole process might appear to be harmless there is no knowing what may be picked up unnoticed, possibly to appear later as gradual and insidious obsession or overshadowing. The whole approach to the unseen of credulous passivity in uncontrolled conditions is one that responsible spiritualists themselves would decry.

Where things could get spectacularly out of hand is where a natural medium, or someone with hysterical or neurotic tendencies fairly near the surface, is by accident one of the company. It is regrettable that ouija and planchette devices have been sold in toy shops in recent years under the guise of party games. Dabbling with unknown forces is no game!

Having established the possibility of making contact with the physically departed, the point now is, where does one go from there? Spiritualists tend to stay at the level of communication between ordinary people on both sides of death. At its most superficial level, as at a public meeting, it is rather like a 'Family Favourites' radio record programme, but without the records. The messages are as short and trite, even if sincerely given and received. More lengthy and intimate communications go on, of course, in private appointments with mediums.

Spiritualism and Occultism

Professional mediumship is a vexed question. Some sincere spiritualists feel that it is not moral to charge money for such consultations and they do it under the aegis of the spiritualist church. There are those, however, who do a flourishing business in such matters. This is not always in the field of communication with the departed. It may be in palmistry, astrology, crystal gazing, card reading or other forms of fortune telling. It is here that we start to go from spiritualism to the occult.

Spiritualism seeks to prove the existence of planes of existence beyond the physical. Occultism takes this for granted and sees how this fact can be best utilized. In the field of communication, rather than spend time conversing with friends or relatives, the occultist seeks out the more 'advanced' soul—the spiritual teacher on the 'inner' planes.

There are various occult organizations or fraternities which would claim, either publicly or privately, to have their base on the 'inner planes' and their members or disciples or students on the physical. They give teaching on the meaning and purpose of life, and the ways and means of what they consider to be spiritual development. Some of these organizations openly advertise for members, while others are more reserved and even secretive, gaining their new members through personal recommendation or from inquirers who have read various books of teaching that they have put out.

Although there are variations of detail, most of them teach broadly similar principles. These for the most part stem from oriental sources, Buddhist or Hindu, even where there is no obvious eastern flavour about the teaching as presented.

Occult Philosophy

For instance, the principle of reincarnation is generally taught, and also karma, together with a detailed analysis of the many and various inner planes and aspects of man and the universe. Practical teaching is also given on meditation with a view to personal spiritual development and eventual personal contact with the 'masters' or 'inner plane adepts' behind the organization.

The western occultist would say that the apparent eastern bias of his teaching is because the 'mystery tradition', which is or was originally one the world over, was stamped out by the persecutions of the Christian church in the west, so that it has only survived in anything like systematic form in the east. Many try to rebuild what they consider to be a valid western system, using western myths, legends and traditions (such as the Arthurian Legends of the Round Table and the Holy Grail), but using for guidance the techniques and theories of the eastern masters of yoga.

Reincarnation is the belief that one is reborn to this life again and again. This is allied to a theory of spiritual evolution of consciousness. There are four conditions of physical existence: mineral, vegetable, animal and human. Consciousness exists in all things, but at its most primitive and in a dreamlike state in the mineral kingdom. Even in the mineral kingdom, however, there is evolution, from simple to complex forms. The highly organized gem stones and crystals, and precious metals, are held to be more evolved parts of the mineral kingdom. Part of this idea is contained in alchemy where it was held that 'base' metals like lead can be helped to evolve to more 'spiritual' metals like silver and gold.

Above the mineral kingdom is the vegetable kingdom, starting from the beginnings of organic life in simple scums and algae, and proceeding to cultivated plants of a high degree of organization like the lily or the rose.

Consciousness proceeds to the next kingdom, that of the animals, where from simple amoeba-like forms it proceeds to that of the higher domestic animals such as the dog and horse.

Then with the development of the moral sense the human kingdom is reached—the difference between human and animal being not only in higher intelligence but in a knowledge of right and wrong.

Some occult systems, such as Theosophy, teach that we have all evolved through all these stages, on this world and on previous worlds, and that we shall continue to evolve until we are great spiritual beings like angels or the spirits behind planets and stars, and eventually gods in our own right. Such a process naturally would be expected to take millions or billions of years.

There is a whole field of fascinating speculation on what life might have been like on previous planets and solar systems, and what it might be like on planets and solar systems yet to come. As astronomers use units of measurement such as light-years to cope with vast distances of inter-stellar space, so do the occultists who speculate in this fashion use especially large units of time, such as the Great Year, during which the sun passes through the entire zodiac in its rising. This is the natural phenomenon of the Precession of the Equinoxes and it takes the sun approximately twenty-four thousand years to go through the cycle. This is one Great Year. We are at present witnessing the sun passing from the sign of Pisces to that of Aquarius—hence the great occult-fringe interest in the

Age of Aquarius, of which many feel themselves to be pioneers, and opposed to the outgoing and outworn standards of the passing Piscean Age, which lasted from about the birth of Christ to the present day.

On a less extended time scale, a mere ten to twenty thousand years ago, there is also fascinating speculation on conditions of life as they were in lost worlds of pre-history, such as Atlantis, allegedly sunk beneath the waves of the Atlantic after great cataclysms caused, it is thought, by abuse of evil powers. And beyond this in time are other lost continents, such as Lemuria or Mu, thought to be probably under the Pacific Ocean.

During the historical period of time, from ancient Egypt to the present, there is also the investigation of the conditions of our own past lives. There are some people who claim to be able to recall them in detail, though it is also taught that such restrospective activity is not always a good thing, any more than dwelling on our own childhood in this life might be, and that we should concentrate upon our present condition with a view to future development.

The essence of this philosophy is that by improving our spiritual stature we eventually achieve release from the wheel of birth and death and become 'just men made perfect'. Until that time we are subject to the Law of Karma which rules that whatever evil we may do has to be repaid in some way, if not in this life, then in a future life. By the same token, any great misfortune in this life is the inevitable result of evil deeds or attitudes in some previous life. By this philosophy it is held that all apparent injustice in the world is explained. Although the wicked may appear to flourish as the green bay tree, they will eventually be brought to book as a natural consequence of their own actions.

A belief developing from this is that every human being has two psychological parts—a Higher Self and a Lower Self. It is the Lower Self that is the personality that we are in everyday life, and which generates or pays for karma. It is a 'projection' of the Higher Self, into which it eventually becomes absorbed after death. The Higher Self then absorbs the experiences of the 'lower worlds' before projecting another Lower Self or personality in course of time. This explains why we normally have no memory of our past lives.

Occult meditation exercises strive to make conscious contact between the Lower and Higher Selves, so that the 'false I' of the personality is replaced by the 'true I' of the more spiritual part of the self. And of course the eventual aim is to have Higher Self consciousness all the time, by which time there is no real need to reincarnate any further.

It is such souls as these that are believed to be the 'Masters' or 'inner plane adepts' or 'secret chiefs' of various occult organizations. These beings, it is held, instead of proceeding to their rest or to further evolution of consciousness on remote planes of existence, elect to stay within the earth sphere to help struggling humanity upon its way. They do this, either by telepathic influence on scientists, politicians and the like, or by running occult schools of teaching, meditation and magic.

Occult Arts

The basic techniques of the occult schools are similar to those of spiritualism in that some kind of telepathic, clairvoyant or clairaudient contact is attempted as a means of communication with those on other planes of existence. The occult type of communication tends to be impersonal and philosophical however, and in some schools lower types of psychism and trance are frowned upon; a direct 'mind to mind' or intuitional contact is preferred. The term 'mediator' is preferred to that of 'medium', and it is held that ideas are presented directly to the mediator's higher consciousness. These are then expressed in the mediator's own words. This is instead of a spirit actually 'controlling' the medium's physical vocal chords or implanting words or pictures into the psychic's imagination.

As well as the basic meditational exercises, such schools tend to offer their students large amounts of printed teachings of a philosophical nature, by which they are expected to regulate their lives. And on the practical side, study of ancient arts and sciences, such as astrology, divination or magic is generally encouraged.

Astrology we have already briefly touched upon in our reference to the Precession of the Equinoxes. It is a study of the apparent motions of the stars and planets, sun and moon, as viewed from earth, in the belief that they either influence or act in parallel to events on earth, as a kind of cosmic clock or mirror. It is a highly complex subject, which is a far cry from the popular 'horoscopes' in the newspapers where only the position of the sun at the time of birth is taken into account. A proper horoscope takes into account not just the position of the sun but of the planets too, and all in relation to a precise geographical point and moment of time— that of physical birth. The complicated star maps that ensue may then be used for character analysis or in an attempt to predict future trends in life.

Divination also has similar ends in view but uses different means. These may be the shuffling and chance distribution of cards (preferably the old Tarot cards, the forerunners of our modern playing cards); the chance pricking of patterns in sand, called geomancy; the chance shuffling of sticks or coins as in the Chinese I Ching; and various other devices ranging from interpreting the lines of the hand (cheiromancy) to the bumps on the head (phrenology). There are also techniques of swinging pendulums, either to dowse for water or minerals, or to answer specific questions. In general, these are all techniques directed to making some conscious contact with the subconscious mind in the hope that *through* the subconscious mind, contact with other worlds may be established.

Magical ritual is less commonly practised as it is held by some to be possibly dangerous, but it is another important way of making contact, through drama and mime plus a vivid use of the creative imagination, with the subconscious mind and beyond. Here, instead of playing with deep symbolism printed on pasteboard (as in Tarot cards), similar symbolism is physically constructed and people act out various roles of symbolic figures or god forms. Obviously this is not very easily organized as a number of people are required, with a large room at their disposal, preferably used solely for that purpose, and which is also soundproof and free from chance disturbance.

A branch of this type of activity is witchcraft, where instead of expensive symbolic furniture such as swords, sceptres, chalices, engraved pentacles and so on, more homely devices are used, such as the knife, the broomstick, the cooking pot or cauldron. There is also a fundamental difference between the attitude of the magician and that of the witch (or wiccan, 'wise one').

The magician is usually more intellectual, deriving his symbolism and belief from complex philosophical ideas about the universe. The witch is closer to nature and rather more inclined to a primitive pagan belief in, and worship of, earth or moon goddess and/or the old horned god of nature. The white witch's interests run traditionally in the field of healing and simple charms and spells. And we should perhaps distinguish between the cult of the 'wicca', with its organized covens, and the individual wiseman or wise-woman dispensing charms and herbs with the additional use of some clairvoyance and fortune telling—though the boundary line is sometimes hard to draw.

The fact that the medieval religious imagination invested the devil with horns, tail and cloven feet, should not cause us automatically to condemn witchcraft as devil worship. The medieval devil borrowed his features from the ancient primeval gods who, though devastatingly out-of-date, are not necessarily evil.

The worship of nature, a heresy which witches tend to fall into, is not intrinsically evil either. It is a worship of a part of God's creation, rather than of God Himself. This is a very different thing from worship of evil, and perhaps less reprehensible than modern suburban man's worship of car, house and possessions.

Similarly, magic is by no means as uniformly black as it is painted. The popular novelist and sensational Sunday journalists have tended to make the ordinary person regard all magic as black magic. That such does exist is true, but there are also white magicians who would abhor being classified in this way.

Black magic is concerned with the use of drugs, corrupt moral practices, sadism, and ruthless exploitation of people in various horrible and subtle ways, such as hypnosis. For instance, a psychic may be hypnotized to travel in the astral body to spy on people or to do some kind of psychic mischief or injury to them. The particularly despicable thing about this is that if things go wrong it is the psychic who gets injured and not the magician controlling her. In any case, the psychic will tend to sink more and more into the control of the magician's will, and this has been known to result in almost complete (and literal) brain-washing—with all will, integrity and self-direction washed away and a human being degraded into a kind of zombie. Hypnosis, like magical ritual, is but a psychological technique and is neither 'good' nor 'evil' in itself. It depends how it is used and for what purpose.

The white magician tries to do good by his work, and may call himself a Christian. Whether he can in fact be so we shall discover in the following sections.

2

WHAT WE HAVE TO SAY

Who are the Spirits ?

THERE are two ways of looking at the claims of the spiritualist and occultist about the existence of supernatural worlds beyond the life we know. One is to refuse to believe in them entirely, and the other is to accept that such worlds exist but to say that the evidence is not being properly assessed.

Disbelief in the existence of any form of life after death is the standpoint of the materialist. And though materialists attack the spiritualist and occultist for unscientific credulity, they attack the Christian on the same grounds. Christians have this much in common then with spiritualists and occultists in that they are also opposed to a materialistic interpretation of life.

Spiritualists in particular feel that they are doing a service for all the Christian churches (and for most other religions, for that matter) in providing evidence that there is no death. They are somewhat disappointed when the orthodox churches give them little thanks or credit for it. Why do the orthodox churches feel this way?

To begin with, although they believe in, and teach, the existence of an after-life, they are not convinced that the after-life contacted by the spiritualists is necessarily the true one.

They would say that it is by no means always a 'spirit' that is contacted in a spiritualist meeting. All that may be happening is that the clairvoyant or medium has a facility for telepathically reading another person's conscious or subconscious mind.

Clairvoyance, or psychism, is an ultra-sensitivity to 'atmosphere'. All but the most insensitive of us is aware of the different 'feel' of different places—the 'over-used' impersonal atmosphere of a railway waiting-room, the massed enthusiasm of a sports stadium, the intense audience reactions in a theatre or cinema. Obviously there are certain physical things in the environment that give some of this feeling—the sights and sounds going on—but there is also something more, a kind of telepathic link or *rapport* with the others there. This can even affect people's behaviour, and it is well known that an individual in a crowd may be capable of doing things, whether of heroism, or stupidity, or cruelty, that he would be incapable of doing on his own.

Certain places, particularly where there has been much emotion generated, especially over a period of time, can affect a sensitive person, whether the place be a church or a dentist's waiting room. In the latter, the nervous feelings one has may not be one's own but a picking-up of the feelings of other people, reinforcing each other in the atmosphere over the years!

The more sensitive one is, and the more imaginative, the worse one may feel, though of course it can work the other way in pleasant circumstances. With some, who are naturally ultra-sensitive, or who have been trained to be, it is possible to pick up actual thoughts, in pictures or words, either from things or from people.

When it is from things, it is a technique known as psychometry. The psychometrist holds an object and is then able to tell something of its history and its previous owners by the pictures that come into his mind.

When it is with people then it is not always what it may seem to be.

It is not unknown for people to be badly deluded by advice given by clairvoyant consultants who think that they are foretelling the future when all the time they have been telepathically picking up the inquirer's hopes and fears and simply telling these back to him. In so far as these hopes and fears are based on real possibilities, then a quite startlingly accurate 'forecast' of the future may seem to be made. But if they are mere wishful fantasies which are hardly likely to come true, like winning a fortune, much harm can result, particularly if financial or business advice is asked for. To play the stock market or the races on clairvoyant advice has yet to be proved a reliable way of making money. It has however proved a spectacular way of losing it. Obviously, if any clairvoyant could predict stock movements or the results of horse races or football matches, they would quickly make themselves a fortune and have no need to give advice about the future for a fee.

When it comes to spiritualism, delusion is all the easier, particularly with recently bereaved folk. In their intense grief they will have built up an image of their lost loved one, charged with all the force of deep emotion, which a clairvoyant may well 'see' with great clarity.

What is not realized is that the 'spirit' so described is not in fact there at all; what is there is only a psychic shell manufactured by the people themselves. It is for this reason that many spiritualistic messages are so trite; they do not come from anybody. It is a longstanding major challenge to spiritualism generally that no literary man who has died has ever managed to pass back a message of anything like the literary quality that he was capable of whilst alive. This suggests either that no really accurate communication by mediumistic means is possible, or else that the whole thing is a delusion coming from the minds of the sitters present.

These are the Christian criticisms of spiritualistic communication that are in part agreement with those of the materialist. It is accepted that extra-sensory perception of various kinds is possible, but whether it is really communication with the dead is doubted. It is thought more likely to be subconscious communication with the living.

Some Christian critics of spiritualism would go further, however, particularly those who have experience of the ministry of exorcism. They may accept the fact that there is communication with spirits but they want to know how it is proved that the spirit is who it claims to be. It is extremely difficult to prove identity accurately, for if telepathy is the means of communication, then even if the medium mentions something known only to the deceased and the sitter, that something could well have been picked up telepathically from the living sitter.

And it might well be that another spirit could be posing as the deceased, out of mischief, malice or idle curiosity. One of the psychic shells we have just mentioned could possibly be taken over or inhabited by another spirit altogether, either human, sub-human or demonic! Who knows exactly what strange fish lurk in these dark metaphysical waters?

Those who think spiritualism is a particularly easy prey to these dangers prefer to call it 'spiritism' on the grounds that, though it may well be dealing with spirits, they are not necessarily very spiritual.

In trying to make an assessment of these matters, we need to define our terms carefully. We must first distinguish between what is religious and what is scientific; and then between what is mystical and what is psychical.

Religion and Science

A religious and scientific muddle comes about because some spiritualists and occultists make a scientific claim about what they are doing. They say that their approach to religion is one of investigation, like any branch of science, though they permit themselves to use subjective means as an extension of the physical scientific methods that are used by such scientific bodies as the Society for Psychical Research.

There can hardly be any Christians who take exception to the extension of human knowledge through scientific investigation, though in fact science does raise certain moral dilemmas. And before Christians raise doubts about the advisability of science trying to investigate 'beyond the grave', we must ask ourselves whether they should not first attend to more crucial moral problems. The power of science to split the atom and cause nuclear devastation is one, but of relatively small significance compared to the problems that arise as man begins to control the processes of life (and even creation?) in biological laboratories, so gaining increased power over death (or the delaying of it). What would happen if the life span were increased to 120? What would happen if we could arrange whether boy or girl babies were born to a mother, particularly in countries where boy babies are esteemed more highly than girls? How long should one postpone an inevitable death in a useless and painful life? Who pays for the drugs to prolong it? Suppose we could create 'character' in unborn children by doctoring their genes? We have problems enough in the offing that dwarf the age-old problem of the investigation of life conditions after death.

However, alongside the scientific approach to spiritualist and occult phenomena there are religious claims. Many regard spiritualism as a religion.

There are no doubt good reasons why this has come about. Those early spiritualist pioneers who heralded the awakening of the spiritualist movement in the nineteenth century almost certainly felt that life after death ought to come into the religious rather than the scientific sphere. And as they might not be sure what kind of spirit they were contacting, they would feel that some kind of ethical or religious composing of the mind should accompany these activities.

Thus it would seem logical to open any such meeting with hymns and prayers or a serious address. And so we have, almost without realizing it, all the trappings of a religious service including, no doubt, the collection! And from the organization of many small meetings of this kind, the formation of a new religious denomination or sect automatically springs up.

However, in this process, things have happened the wrong way round! It is rather like a pious biologist thinking that his experiments into the nature of life are as much a matter of religion as of science, and starting all his experiments with a hymn and a prayer. There is nothing wrong with this in itself, but what happens if he starts giving public lectures and demonstrations of (say) the formation of cell cultures, all accompanied with the trappings of a religious service?

It could well happen that, by insidious degrees, the cell cultures become not the object of reverent investigation, but the object of worship. And here lies a danger of spiritualism. Because communications from the dead are received in a religious setting, they tend to be unconsciously regarded as edicts from God. But if so, this is a reversion to primitive ancestor worship no matter how 'Christian' the hymns and prayers may be.

So, whilst no one would wish to avoid an attitude of reverence in such investigations, rather than a kind of callous psychological vivisection of the departed in the name of 'science', there are plainly great spiritual dangers looming.

This is particularly so with those who have just been tragically bereaved, clinging to any straw for some kind of proof of survival of their loved one, at a time when their Christian faith is at a considerable test.

We do not say that responsible spiritualists are unaware of these dangers. They do exist and there are probably more than many would care to admit, though the reason they exist may also be a measure of the Christian church's failure to exercise the whole of its ministry, as we shall see later.

Psychism and Mysticism

The other area where we need to define our terms carefully relates closely to this danger of losing true Christian faith for inner peace at any price, and this is in the difference between psychism and mysticism.

There is considerable confusion between these two terms, not made easier because they may overlap. The area of overlap is, however, small, and the main problem is that most people do not realize that there is in fact a profound difference between them. They tend to use the word 'mystical' simply as an alternative to magical or psychical phenomena.

The word 'mystical' refers, however, to a direct relationship to God, the Creator. The word 'psychical' refers to a direct relationship with other created beings, albeit on other levels of creation.

The word 'magical' follows from this, and refers to a technique or science of handling various subtle forces that you have been made aware of through psychism, or occasionally through mysticism.

Drugs such as LSD, or mescalin, have the property of opening up consciousness psychically, hence their attraction for those of little worldly achievement or ambition. These, linked to a will too weak to undertake a proper discipline of psychical and magical training, as in yoga or its western occult equivalents, seem to some an easy way to get some kind of psychical results. The required effort may be small, but at what a price!

It is doubly unfortunate too that in some books these drug experiences are referred to as 'mystical'. There is in fact little of God in them, however transcendent the feelings induced by taking them may be. And in extreme cases you find growing up 'psychedelic churches', which castigate the orthodox church for lack of 'results', in terms of religious experience.

But the church does not in the least lack its results, although, as we shall examine in our next part, it may have underplayed and underestimated its mystical heritage disastrously, thus giving the opportunity to these cults to spring up, false in their teaching, delusory in their 'results', but fulfilling (if in an inadequate and dangerous fashion) a genuine need.

Take the journals or records of great mystics of the church from Paul onwards. Many of them were surrounded at times by remarkable phenomena: Teresa d'Avila levitated, Francis of Assisi had the stigmata, Fox the Quaker is reported to have 'glowed', John Vianney was clearly clair-

voyant and prophetic, and subject at times to violent poltergeistic phenomena such as would be the envy of any psychical researcher or occult
dabbler. But all go on record ,when they speak of such matters, as saying
that such psychical things are of no consequence and that little attention
should be paid to them.

Magic, White and Black

We have mentioned magic as a particular development springing princi-
pally from psychism, or that uses psychism in its workings. Again we have
confusion over use of terms.

To most modern people brought up in our present intellectual climate
of all-powerful science and technology—and this includes a large majority
of church people, including ordained ministers—the thought of magic is
quite ludicrous. It is regarded as outworn superstition. But those few
whose spiritual vocation is the ministry of exorcism know differently.
Unfortunately, the experience of magic that most exorcists have is often
of the worst possible kind. That is, they are called in to try and clean up
after someone has made a sordid mess of things.

For instance, groups of people hire a secluded cottage and perform old
rituals, misunderstood and taken from old medieval grimoires (magical
recipe books), perhaps half in jest, and then they find too late that there is
'something in it' after all—and that that something may be something
very nasty.

Certainly a pantomime demon king does not jump up through the
floorboards holding a trident in a puff of green smoke! But the mind is a
little-understood thing, and only those who have experienced it can know
the peculiar horror of a psychic obsession or an overshadowing by unknown forces—forces that insidiously undermine and even obliterate all
sense of personal identity, let alone integrity. Something of such powers,
and how closely they verge on clinical psychotic or neurotic states, can be
appreciated safely at second hand by fictional descriptions such as Henry
James's *The Turn of the Screw*, which has been made into a spine-chilling
film called *The Innocents*.

This is black magic. It can be all of what is described in popular occult
novels, but without the glamour. The actual powers are not as physical

and obvious as they may be described in fiction. No one is likely to be physically rebuffed by a pentagram to the extent of feeling he has walked into an invisible rubber wall. But the forces can be as effectively dangerous because they are more subtle. As germs of physical disease can be picked up without a person noticing the fact at the time, so the same applies to psychical or occult disease. The results are no more pleasant either.

But there do exist white magicians, who genuinely abhor the traffic in drugs, sadism and sexual perversion that goes with black magic cults. White magicians, however, are rather rare birds. They do not seek to recruit, and pursue their unusual spiritual vocations in or outside the church according to an inner call.

Their work is closely akin to prayer, and what we shall have to say in our next section will show that their techniques could perhaps usefully be put to more general use by the church.

There are, however, those outside the church, who consider themselves to be white magicians (and in this category we could also include 'white witches') but who, for various reasons, eschew Christianity, preferring the old pagan or classical religious formulations, and perhaps deriving their religious and philosophical ideas from the east. Some openly claim that there is no difference between Christian and non-Christian worship if properly understood—that all religions are simply different ways of worshipping the one God.

This sounds very reasonable, and highly ecumenical. It is, indeed, true so far as it goes; but to the Christian it does not really go far enough.

Christian or Pagan

There is in fact a profound difference between Christian and pagan creeds. The religions of man before Christ came to earth were but man's ideas (often very spiritual and ethical) about what God might be. The incarnation of Christ and all that led up to it through a thousand years and more of Jewish history was, however, a *revelation* of what God *is*.

There is nothing necessarily evil about pagan religions therefore, whether they are the ancient primitive semi-superstitious rites of tribal man or the more sophisticated philosophical flights of thought of ancient Greece, Egypt, China or India. They are genuine approaches of man toward God, even if they are apt to wander sometimes in a wrong direction.

However, the fact that their myths are in some respects so similar to the life of Jesus (the sacrifice of the redeeming hero who saves the world, for instance) does show that man has always had natural glimmerings of the ways of God, and that God could speak to man through man's own sub-conscious yearnings for the divine.

Christians have tended to undervalue the pagan creeds because of the special historical mission of the Jews as the 'chosen race' to embody the incarnation. It was important in the eyes of the Old Testament prophets that the Jews should evolve their religious beliefs in ways separate from those of the surrounding tribes.

Therefore we must realize that the occultist, who, going further than the spiritualist, uses non-Christian religious philosophies to support his views of life after death, is not necessarily being evil, but simply very much out-of-date and guilty of leaving out a whole dimension of reality. And this in spite of the fact that he thinks he is custodian of wider dimensions than the Christian. He is concerned entirely with the speculations of man, perhaps refined to a very high and spiritual degree, but he is ignoring God's personal revelation to man.

The same thing applies whether we are taking the instance of the witch, (who goes back to primitive forms of nature worship), or the theosophist (who makes philosophical extensions on to the beliefs of certain schools of Buddhism and Hinduism). What they are putting forward as new ideas that hold more truth than the Christian religion are in fact old ideas con-taining less.

It may well be that Christians do not present their case properly and therefore appear to be more old-fashioned and limited in their views than these older religions, but that is another matter.

Spiritualism and Jesus

Other spiritualists claim that the resurrection of Jesus Christ is evidence for the existence of the 'astral body' or 'ghost'. Some clergymen, who ought to know better, have even accepted this line. But what the gospels bear witness to are hardly phenomena of this nature.

When Jesus appeared to the disciples on the road to Emmaus, for example, it was in broad daylight and not in the dim lights and carefully controlled conditions of a spiritualist séance.

Furthermore, on at least one occasion when He was with the disciples in His resurrected body He joined in a meal with them. As, for instance, in Luke 24: 36–43. 'As they were talking about all this, there he was, standing among them. Startled and terrified, they thought they were seeing a ghost. But he said, "Why are you so perturbed? Why do questionings arise in your minds? Look at my hands and feet. It is I myself. Touch me and see; no ghost has flesh and bones as you can see that I have." They were still unconvinced, still wondering, for it seemed too good to be true. So he asked them, "Have you anything here to eat?" They offered him a piece of fish they had cooked, which he took and ate before their eyes.' There is no record of any astral visitant eating physical food. Likewise, when he wished, He was solid to the physical touch, as when He invited doubting Thomas to feel the wounds of the crucifixion.

The Christian would therefore hold that the life after death demonstrated by Jesus was unique in that it is a foreshadowing of what is possible to all who repent and believe in the Christ as Son of God and Son of Man. It has nothing to do with the evidence of psychic phenomena or mediumistic powers.

Jesus had shown forth the state of the 'new life' in His transfiguration . on the mountainside before His death. There, before Peter, James and John, He had suddenly appeared radiant, His flesh, His hair, and His clothes glowing white and dazzling, to the accompaniment of other wonders.

Later, after His death on the cross, His physical body disappeared. In no case of spiritualist phenomena is there evidence of the astral body being formed from a reconstituted physical body.

When He appeared to His disciples in His resurrection body, it had powers that transcended the physical laws of nature. He could appear, disappear, be solid to the touch, recognizable or unrecognizable, be present to few or to many (five hundred at a time according to Paul), and finally ascend into a cloud as a sign that the mission to man was over, and that the Holy Spirit would henceforward guide the church in its ways, after its manifestation at Pentecost in tongues of fire and a rushing wind.

Therefore, whatever the merits of spiritualist communicators may be, they are not of the type that was shown forth by Jesus. The members of the early church did not have to be psychic to communicate with Him. Rather, what was needed was not psychic development, but 'repentance' —a change in direction of the selfish will of man back to obedience to the will of God.

Through baptism, man acknowledged this repentance, and his belief that God had revealed Himself to man through Jesus and given mankind the opportunity to wipe out the fruits of his own inbred sinfulness. By turning the will towards conformity with the will of God, death could not be avoided, but it could be endured and survived, not as a bodiless personality but as a new being on a new 'wavelength'. It would be a condition that mankind had originally fallen from, and which he recalled as a Golden Age or Garden of Eden, but which later came to be called by John the Divine the New Jerusalem. That is, a world as it should have been, had not man's will turned from God in disobedience, at the behest (according to legend) of a fallen angel.

The opportunity for this new life was given by God through the mission of Jesus, and the importance of this mission was that Jesus took up (or restored) manhood into God-head. Thus the fundamental importance of Jesus the Christ's saying, 'I am the way, the truth, and the life' and 'No one cometh to the Father but by me.'

Occult students do not always realize this, and vainly seek for other ways. It is to their loss.

3

WHAT WE HAVE TO LEARN

The 'Inner' Creation

WHEN the Christian church was newly founded it had a great struggle with forms of pagan thought and speculation. Even though it brought many religious pagans within its fold, they were apt to keep the same basic ideas as once they held before they believed in Christ.

The problem exercised the church for several centuries, and when the Christian church became the reigning religion in the Roman Empire it was not slow to use physical persecution to help it establish its creed. Though this is to be regretted, the church is made of human beings, and humans are fallible creatures.

In their desire to retain the truth in as pure a form as they could, the Early Fathers tended to go too far, and so much valuable pagan speculation was lost to the world. This speculation in its Christian form was known as Gnosticism (those who had knowledge), a special knowledge of God by means of various special beliefs and practices.

This was firmly rejected by the early church, which rightly said that Christ came for all men and not just for a few who banded themselves together in secret societies. And Gnostics did tend to miss the point of the incarnation of Jesus Christ, with their preoccupation with higher worlds, and heavenly beings, and angelic hierarchies. Their members went through complex initiation ceremonies, and learned strings of passwords and words of power to help their passage through the heaven worlds, whereas the church taught that all that was needed for salvation was repentance and belief in Christ.

Anyhow, as a consequence of orthodox zeal and Gnostic excesses, the movement was effectively stamped out. Unfortunately, stamping out is not an ideal solution to any human difference of opinion, however misguided the opinions may seem to those who do the stamping. The very existence of the opinion suggests that there is a human need that it answers; and the existence of a human need unfulfilled hints at the existence of neglected truths.

It is true that subsequently the church did start to build up a kind of plan of the 'inner' creation that had once been such a happy hunting ground for the Gnostics. This plan or pattern was built up through the work of the great thinkers of the early church such as Augustine of Hippo and Thomas Aquinas, and the whole metaphysical edifice that was so built reached its height in the literary expression of Dante's *Divine Comedy* in about 1300.

When the medieval world view broke up, through the advance of various scientific and social impulses, Dante's vision fell into neglect, and probably only its standing as great poetic literature enabled it to survive and remain accessible to all. (A translation is available in Penguin books.)

However, although to the superficial eye it may appear to be invalid because it is based on a symbolism of seven heavens and crystalline spheres about the earth, with hell down below in the centre of the earth, purgatory at the antipodes, and heaven out in space, all of which (as physical concepts) have been exploded by modern science, a very great point has been missed. Although the outer physical symbolism may have altered, the inner reality it describes may very well be valid.

Those who desire to speculate deep upon the mysteries of God and the universe, and who find little to help or guide them in the modern church, could do far worse than to study Dante.

It is a tough and difficult discipline, as might be expected, for trying to understand the complexities of the universe (even if man's mind is capable of it) is not likely to be so easy as learning the multiplication table. The *Divine Comedy* may also seem theologically suspect to some members of Protestant or Reformed Churches but, if it is read as psychology rather than theology, most differences become, on close reading, superficial. And Dante's vision is certainly theologically and psychologically more accurate than most forms of occult and spiritualist speculation, and is based on the reasoned beliefs of some of the most formidable intellects the Christian church has produced.

It is a great book describing one of the two ways to direct knowledge of God, the Positive Way (or *via positiva*) as opposed to the Negative Way (or *via negativa*).

The Positive Way builds up a great complex of symbols as a means of conveying to the soul what God is. These images may vary considerably but in Dante they centre in two great concepts: the image of a beloved city (Florence) and the image of a beloved girl (Beatrice). He saw God as a fair city from which man had been exiled as he himself was exiled from Florence; and he also saw God as being like a long-lost passionate love, as Dante had loved, from a distance, Beatrice Fortinari.

There is a certain daring about this imagery (particularly in comparing a young girl to God) so that Dante at first, in spite of his orthodoxy, suffered some censorship at the hands of the medieval church. But it is no more strange than likening God to a city, or for that matter to a burning bush, as in the Bible, or to the time-honoured popular image of an old man in a white nightgown which may have been the only way to present God to children but which has been a stumbling-block to many struggling not very successfully to 'put away childish things'.

God is, in His essence, and in spite of having approached man through Christ, so 'other' from man that any image of Him we try to construct must be distorted or incomplete. 'Why prate ye of God?' said Meister Eckhart, a great mystic, 'All that ye can say of him is untrue!'

From this difficulty in the Positive Way, the Negative Way obtains its logic. Since God cannot be described fully by any one image, why try to use any image at all? *The Cloud of Unknowing*, a famous early English mystical textbook (also available in Penguin), sets out to approach God in this fashion, simply by wanting to enter 'the dark cloud' that is God, or of which, to revert to an image again, God is the silver lining. So its anonymous author recommends simply selecting a name or a word to represent the soul's need for God, and repeating it over and again, with feeling. It is not far from the practice of Jesus, who enjoins us to look upon God simply as a loving Father.

The Negative Way has been too long neglected in the western churches, though the eastern Orthodox Churches have retained a considerable regard for and practice of it, possibly because in their system of church government only monks can become bishops.

The way of *The Cloud of Unknowing* is also similar to what yoga exponents would call 'mantra yoga', but it is considerably more besides. And there is, in fact, little in Christendom that occultism has to teach it. Where occultism and spiritualism can be of help is in reminding the church of certain jewels within its rich spiritual treasure chest that the church seems to have forgotten.

The Problem of Prayer

This forgotten heritage is more of a general problem than is often sufficiently realized. It is not simply a question of trying to cater for a few eccentrics who have a predilection for metaphysical speculation or for dabbling in psycho/spiritual thrills. A massive sort of dry rot affects the church in its members, which is every bit as disastrous as the actual wood disease that attacks the timbers of some of its buildings. And this is the generally complete and utter neglect of teaching people how to pray.

There is in fact least trouble at the two extremes of the Positive and Negative Way. The Positive Way is found especially in the religious pomp and ceremonial of the Catholic service, where prayer is expressed as much in action as in thought and mind. The Negative Way is found in the Quaker meeting, where all present simply sit in silence, 'waiting upon God', until someone may be moved by the Holy Spirit to speak.

Between these two extremes (which, to anyone who has experienced both, are very close together, like the extreme ends of a necklace) is the great broad mass of the church with its members stumbling on as best they may. A putting of the hand in front of the eyes and a rather self-consciously trying to string together some confused recollections of child-hood prayers or odd petitions is the probable way of most. Though this may seem enough for those who are drawn to the church by other ties, social or psychological, it is not enough for those who come to church as a means of a living meeting with God.

It is these that drift away and either seek satisfaction in occultism or other religious sects, or join the great mass of the public who genuinely

33

think that the church is 'a good thing' but never go near it themselves because in practice, apart from major existential crises in life like birth, marriage, and death, they find it irrelevant.

Some may have had genuine spontaneous religious experiences which have brought them to try various churches, only to find that their experience was not nurtured or fulfilled by what the church apparently had to offer. Occult societies, far from being dens of perverse souls of iniquitous intent, as Christian opinion (which for some odd reason apparently gets its lead from the most lurid newspapers and paperback novels) seems to think, are, in fact, full of genuinely and naturally religious people, many of whom have tried to approach the church and been repelled by it. It is all very sad. The church loses great potential support, and when people are driven away, they drift widely astray, following their own fancies without the necessary guidance and discipline of a theologically well-informed ministry.

How then do we teach contemplation and the interior life that intimately 'knows' God? One difficulty is that this Christian heritage has been so neglected that the only works of practical importance are of medieval origin and addressed to full-time contemplatives, the monks and nuns of their own times, whose problems, attitudes and circumstances are very different from those of men and women living in the world today.

The answers are beginning to be provided, outside the church, on the one hand, by the techniques of psychotherapy (which at times verge close to religion), and also by occult schools coming into the open in the modern climate of free exchange of opinion. What psychologists discover and occultists reveal are in fact often ways of the devout life that have been known to the church for centuries but which have been neglected and forgotten.

What is really needed to cure the malaise of the church of the twentieth century is not so much a striving to find something new (by way of revised liturgies or syncopated hymns) but a re-appraisal and stewardship of that which is old.

The psychotherapeutic techniques of which we talk lead, at best, to a re-integration of a damaged personality. The occult meditation techniques lead, at best, to a deeper knowledge of the interior parts of the soul. This is good, but why not go further and integrate them into that from which they should never have been divorced, the prayerful approach of the soul to God?

There are similarities here to a form of visual prayer once formulated by Ignatius of Loyola. His *Spiritual Exercises* have for centuries been the backbone and training of the powerful and spiritually tough priests of the Jesuit Order. But again Ignatius of Loyola is an historical personage speaking to men of his own time, and, though still relevant to certain Roman Catholics with a particular spiritual vocation, his approach is of small use to the average modern Christian. We lack modern works of a similar stature.

As General Booth, the founder of the Salvation Army said when he organized his songsters and brass bands, 'Why should the devil have all the best tunes?' Similarly, why should the techniques of the prayer life be left to yogis, occultists and psychoanalysts who, leaving out the Christ, forget the baby and peddle the bathwater as a cure for souls!

Anthony Duncan's recent book, *The Lord of the Dance*, goes some way to redress the balance, presenting a Christian approach of the soul to God in the form of a series of visualizations in the creative imagination which can lead the soul on to effective prayer. It has also been expressed in other terms in F. C. Happold's *The Journey Inwards*.

'Whole' Christianity

Such exercises are capable of filling a vast gap left by the Christian church's neglect of instruction in prayer. And even where such instruction is given, it is often in a formalized way that, while it may help some, leaves others completely unassisted.

This type of symbolic prayer may be seen as a Christian redemption of certain types of yoga or occultism, but, in fact, it is not so much this as a re-assertion and rediscovery of what was already the Christian church's heritage, which has been neglected and forgotten. Where the church neglects and forgets things, there will the schismatic sects spring up, proclaiming in an unbalanced way those truths of the Holy Spirit that the church has failed to take into its ministry.

Given the fullness of Christian teaching and witness, and the development of all that it implies, there would be no need, no place, for any schismatic sect. In the case of occultism and spiritualism, their existence stems entirely from the church's neglect of the reality of the 'inner' creation and the mystical insights of the contemplative life.

Our aim has been not just to point a finger at some failings of the modern church but also to indicate some possible ways of helping to put things to rights.

One organization within the Anglican church which seems to be moving on these lines is the Servers of Christ the King. They are members of a congregation who meet regularly for a period of silent prayer, somewhat after the fashion of the Quakers, and who, as a result of their prayer, decide what special work needs to be done by them in the parish. In this way, prayer gradually becomes a springboard for action, and not a formal petitioning sandwiched between hymns and sermons, which from school-days onwards is the only type of 'prayer life' that many nominal Christians experience.

It is the lack of the reality of prayer that causes so many souls to drift away from Christianity; a whole area of their being is unfulfilled. And they may commence a sad fallen shadowy copy of the True Quest, hawking themselves round to every occult or spiritualistic society or church in turn, looking for 'truth'.

There is only one Way, Truth and Life; and though some churches may be unduly fixed in their own formulations of what they think the light of the world may be, sooner or later all must return, or come, to Christ as He *is*.

4

POINTS TO REMEMBER

THERE are several ways in which you may be asked to take part in spiritualist activities and they fall under four main headings:

(a) as an exciting game in a party spirit;

(b) as a serious scientific investigation, to see if 'there's anything in it';

(c) as a means to renew communication with deceased loved ones;

(d) as a means to seek a deeper meaning to life.

Before committing yourself to any action you will be wise to consider exactly what you are being asked to do, and a guide to this will be to identify your motive. Why are you doing it?

In the first instance it may be to avoid being thought 'chicken' or 'square' if you refuse. If this is your motive, it does not really say much for your qualities of character or leadership, does it? All who have any experience of such matters, whether they be Christians, spiritualists or occultists, are agreed that to go in for spiritualistic or occult experiments in a frivolous spirit is not only stupid but possibly dangerous. So the same criteria apply as for any other unwise action that you may be prevailed upon to join in just to keep in with the rest of the gang or current social 'herd'.

In categories (a) and (b), curiosity is an important motive, and curiosity is a double-edged natural instinct. Seriously directed curiosity has led man towards many fields of genuine discovery, particularly in the sciences, and it is for this reason that one way of attracting people to spiritualism is by appealing to 'scientific investigation'.

But you need to ask yourself: Is scientific investigation best carried out by people with no scientific training, in their own homes, with casual acquaintances as their fellow researchers? If results of scientific investigation are wanted, vast quantities of them can be consulted at the offices of the Society for Psychical Research. Are you really likely to add to the body of human knowledge by your own home activities? You might as well attempt to discover something of value to chemical science with a home chemistry set.

Therefore let us disabuse ourselves of the idea of assisting the progress of science in this matter. That is only adding pride and delusion to the curiosity we started off with.

If it is 'idle curiosity' that prompts you to look into these things, then at least be aware of that fact, and give a thought to who it is who proverbially finds work for idle hands!

With regard to category (c), we may have an emotional motivation, which can be very strong. But here we need an even closer inspection of our motives. Is such a 'calling back' of loved ones, even if it does not prove to be the delusion of playing with thought forms, really an act of love? Or is it at root a selfish desire for our own emotional comfort?

These are deep and grave matters that fortunately do not come to most of us while we are young, and some considerable life experience is needed to sort out the good from the bad, the real from the spurious. C. S. Lewis, in his somewhat harrowing book *A Grief Observed*, has recorded what such suffering through personal loss may be like, even to a committed Christian. And the pursuit of the dead through mediums can in most cases, one feels, only keep open old and painful wounds.

On the other hand, there is no reason why there should not still be links of mutual love through Christ. The doctrine of what is sometimes called the Communion of Saints (and in Paul's use of the term, the word 'saint' applies to all Christians), and elsewhere the Fellowship of the Holy Spirit, is that we are all part of an inter-communicating organism, the Body of Christ.

If it is so willed, there may be quite unexpected and uncalled for 'evidences' of the continued existence of one's loved ones, human or even animal. But such occurrences come quite unexpectedly—'the Spirit bloweth where it listeth'—and are more likely to come to those who wait and accept their condition in faith than to those who frantically seek for mediumistic channels of communication.

Spiritualists may genuinely feel that they give comfort in such cases, but where it is not comfort through delusion, we need to wonder if it is not at the cost of injury in other respects, particularly to faith.

It is understandable, if regrettable, that those with no Christian belief should resort to such activities, but it is tragic that a Christian should have so little sense of the reality of the Risen Christ that he should attempt to drag back his brothers and sisters in Christ from the deeper unity with their Lord than was possible in physical life.

The same sense of regret must be felt for those who go to Spiritualism for 'a deeper meaning to life', especially for those who have had an ostensibly Christian background and upbringing.

We are here dealing with our fourth category of reasons, (d), and it applies to occultism particularly, because those who go to spiritualism for a deeper meaning to life are generally of an intellectual turn of mind that will not be satisfied for long with the teachings of spiritualism.

Their search may be a lengthy one, for occult teachings of the various schools are exceedingly complex, and one finds many occult students over a period of years going from school to school, having mastered the cosmological teachings of each one and finding them wanting in some respect.

To those who have this restless metaphysical itch we need to ask if they have really considered the teachings of Christ and the church in an adult and unbiased way. If not, by doing so they might save themselves a somewhat prolonged and devious circular tour.

Short Reading List

C. S. Lewis, *Miracles* (Fontana).
C. S. Lewis, *Mere Christianity* (Fontana).
C. S. Lewis, *The Great Divorce* (Bles).
Frank Morison, *Who Moved the Stone?* (Faber).
J. B. Phillips, *Your God is Too Small* (Epworth).
J. B. Phillips, *Ring of Truth* (Hodder & Stoughton).
F. C. Happold, *The Journey Inwards* (Darton, Longman & Todd).
Anthony Bloom, *School for Prayer* (Darton, Longman & Todd).
Anthony Duncan, *The Lord of the Dance* (Helios Book Service).

The fictional works of C. S. Lewis (Penguin), Charles Williams (Faber), and George Macdonald (Penguin), contain much Christian truth in the guise of science fiction, fairy tale, or occult thriller. Dante's *Divine Comedy* and the anonymous *Cloud of Unknowing* (both available in Penguin) are tough going, though very rewarding to the dedicated.